VERTEBRATE ANIMALS

Planet Earth is full of animals.

It is necessary to classify them in order to study them.

Animals can be classified in a number of ways. The most common classification is the one that divides them into two groups, depending on the internal structure of their body:

- **Vertebrate animals:** those that have an internal skeleton made up of bones.

- **Invertebrate animals:** those that do not have an internal skeleton (they do not have bones).

In this book, we will learn everything about vertebrate animals, which are all those that have an articulated **internal skeleton**.

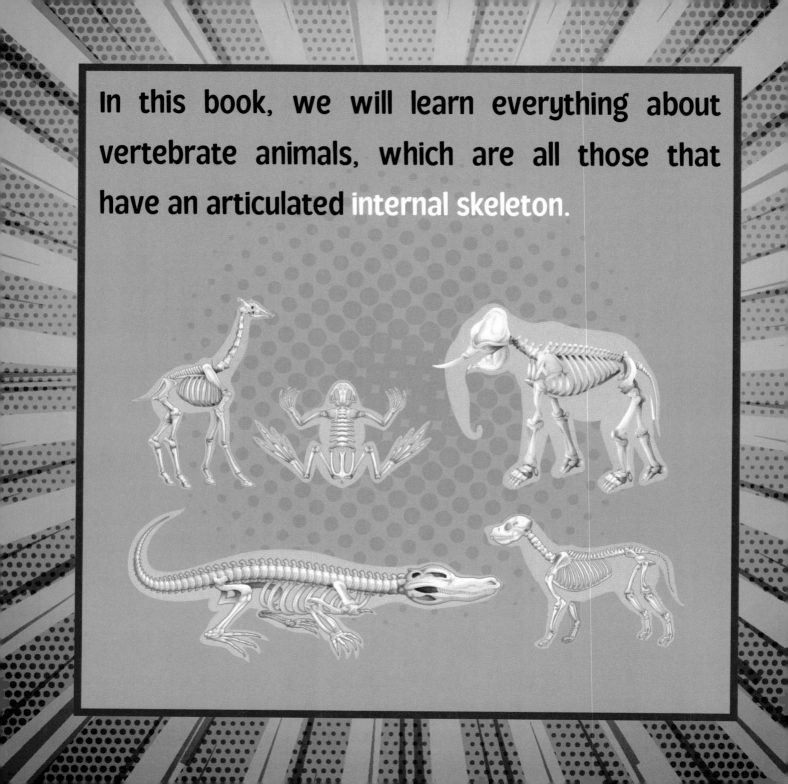

Bones are rigid and strong.

They support the body and give it shape.

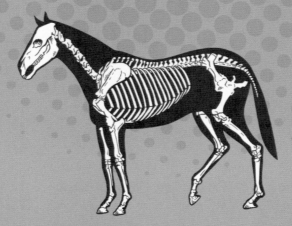

MAMMALS

We, humans, belong to the group of mammals.

Just like us, the rest of the mammals are also viviparous. They are born from their mother's wombs.

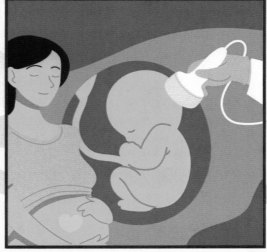

Mammals breathe through their lungs.

Marine mammals also have lungs even if they live in the water (whale, dolphin, seal...).

Mammals are warm-blooded animals.

Homeotherms (warm-blooded) animals keep their bodies at an approximately constant temperature, despite the environment temperature.

Mammals can be classified into three types depending on the environment in which they inhabit:

Terrestrial: they live on land.

Marine: they live in the water.

Volant: they live in caves and up in the trees (they can fly).

Most mammals have their bodies covered with hair.

Many of them are covered with fur. This helps them to keep warm and prevents moisture from reaching the skin.

Some marine mammals, such as the seal, also have their bodies covered with hair.

SUMMARY

- They are viviparous.

- They breathe through their lungs.

- They are warm-blooded.

- Most of them have their bodies covered with hair.

- There are terrestrial, marine, and volant mammals.

DID YOU KNOW...?

- The largest animal on the planet is a mammal, the blue whale, which can grow up to 30 meters in length and weigh more than 100 tons.

- Before they are born, the whale´s body is covered with a layer of hair called lanugo.

- Bats are the only mammals capable of flying, although some types of squirrels and marsupials are capable of gliding in the air.

- Polar bears are not white, in fact, their skin is black. Their hair is hollow and transparent, but we see it white because of an optical effect when light reflects on it.

Birds walk on two legs and have wings that allow them to fly.

Their bones are hollow and filled with air. This makes their skeleton very light so they can fly.

Some birds, such as the ostrich or the penguin, cannot fly despite having wings.

Birds are oviparous animals. That is, they hatch from eggs.

Laying hens can lay about 300 eggs a year.

Ostrich eggs are the largest of all eggs in the world, which can grow up to 10" (25 cm) and weigh up to 4.5 lb (2 kg)!

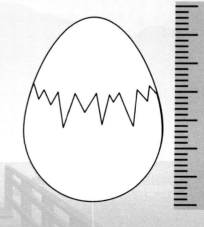

Birds breathe through their lungs just like mammals do.

However, their respiratory system is somewhat different. Air first passes through their air sacs, which store it and pump it into their lungs. This allows birds to breathe despite the effort that staying in flight requires.

Birds are homeotherm animals.

Just like mammals, they are warm-blooded animals. They can keep their body temperature constant regardless of the outside temperature.

Their bodies are covered with feathers.

Bird feathers make flight possible, help maintain their body temperature, and allow them to float on water.

SUMMARY

- **They are** oviparous.

- **They breathe through their** lungs.

- **They are** warm-blooded.

- **They have their bodies covered with** feathers.

- **They have two** wings **that allow them to fly.**

DID YOU KNOW...?

- Some birds can repeat the words and sounds they hear (parrots, cockatoos...).
- The ostrich is the largest bird in the world. It can weigh up to 330 lb (150 kg) and reach a height of 10 ft (3 m).
- The smallest bird is the zunzuncito, some sort of hummingbird that only measures about 2" (5 cm).
- The fastest animal is the peregrine falcon, capable of flying at almost 250 mph (400 km/h).
- Although birds do not have teeth, chicks are born with one that falls out after a few days and helps to break the eggshell.

FISH

Fish are animals that live in the water. They can live in freshwater (rivers, streams, lakes, and lagoons) or saltwater (seas and oceans).

Caudal fin

They use their fins and tail, called the caudal fin, to move through the water.

Most fish are oviparous animals, that is, they hatch from eggs.

There are also viviparous fish, as the example of some sharks, in which the young are born directly from the mother. Others are ovoviviparous, and the eggs hatch inside the mother.

Fish also need oxygen to breathe. They do this through their gills.

- The water enters the fish's mouth.
- Passes through the gills, where oxygen is collected.
- The water is expelled to the outside through the opercular slits.

Fish are cold-blooded animals. Their temperature adapts to the environment.

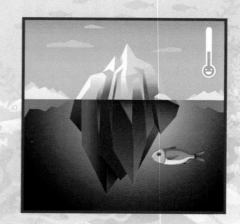

They must be able to withstand all kinds of temperatures. They are hot when it is hot and cold when the temperatures drop.

Most fish have their bodies covered with scales.

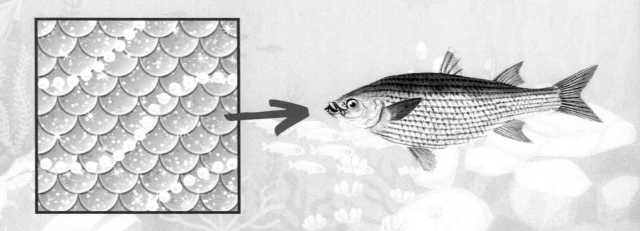

The scales protect them from predators, preventing physical damage, and also serve as a barrier against parasites.

SUMMARY

- They are oviparous.

- They breathe through their gills.

- They are cold-blooded.

- Their bodies are covered with scales.

- They have fins for swimming.

DID YOU KNOW...?

- Some fish, like salmon, can live in both fresh and salt water.
- Fish do not have eyelids. They always have their eyes open. That's why it looks like they never sleep, even though they do. They just move away to rest in some safe corner.
- Some fish can fly. They reach high speeds underwater, propel themselves out of the water, and manage to hover at distances of up to 1,300 ft (400 m).
- The largest fish in the world is the whale shark, which can grow up to 39 ft (12 m).
- The stonefish is the most venomous fish in the world.

Amphibians are oviparous animals, that is, they hatch from eggs.

Amphibian eggs are not covered by a protective shell and are at risk of drying out. That is why the mothers lay their eggs in the water.

Amphibians are born in water, so the young breathe through their gills, just like fish do.

Gills

Lungs

When they become adults, amphibians go through a process called metamorphosis, lose their gills, and develop lungs.

Therefore, in the first stage of their lives, they live entirely in the water. As adults, they spend most of their time on land.

The vast majority of amphibian species have their habitat (the place where they live) near lakes, ponds, or rivers.

Amphibians are cold-blooded animals.

In the same way as fish, and as also applies to reptiles, the temperature of amphibians varies depending on environmental conditions.

Amphibians have bare and moist skin.

- They have no hair, scales, or feathers.
- They can breathe through their skin (cutaneous respiration).
- Some species secrete toxic substances through the skin.

SUMMARY

- They are **oviparous**.

- They **breathe** through **gills, lungs, and their skin**.

- They are **cold-blooded**.

- Their skin is **bare** and **moist**.

- They live in the **water** and on **land**.

DID YOU KNOW...?

- The word amphibian comes from the Greek word *amphibious*. The Greek prefix *amphi* means "both", or "double", and the Greek word *bios* mean "life". The name refers to their two lives, in the water, and on land.

- The Chinese giant salamander grows nearly 6 feet in length (1.8 m) and weighs more than 110 lb (50 kg). It is the largest amphibian in the world.

- The golden frog is the most poisonous animal in the world. A single dose would be capable of killing more than 1500 adults.

- Some frogs have lateral membranes that allow them to get around gliding between trees.

REPTILES

Reptiles are oviparous animals, that is, they hatch from eggs.

Reptile eggs resemble bird eggs. They differ from amphibian and fish eggs because they have a shell that protects them.

Most reptiles are terrestrial. They like to live in warm places, so it is rare to see them in winter.

Their breathing is done through their lungs.

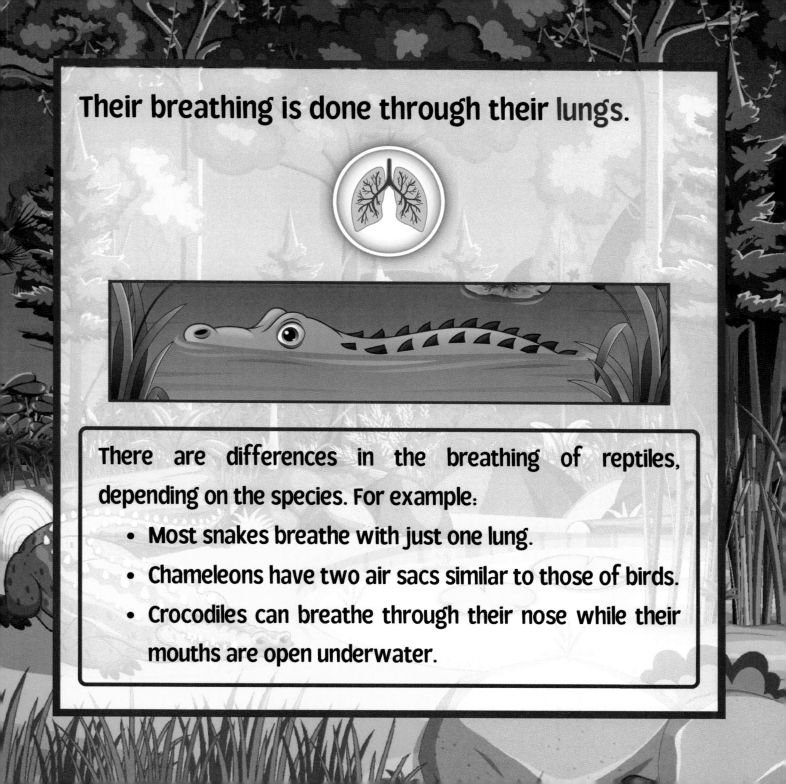

There are differences in the breathing of reptiles, depending on the species. For example:

- Most snakes breathe with just one lung.
- Chameleons have two air sacs similar to those of birds.
- Crocodiles can breathe through their nose while their mouths are open underwater.

Reptiles are cold-blooded animals as well.

Although they are cold-blooded, they need heat to live. Their metabolism changes depending on the temperature of their environment. They are more active when it is hot and less when it is cold. That is why it is common to see crocodiles, lizards, and snakes sunbathing.

Their body is covered with scales.

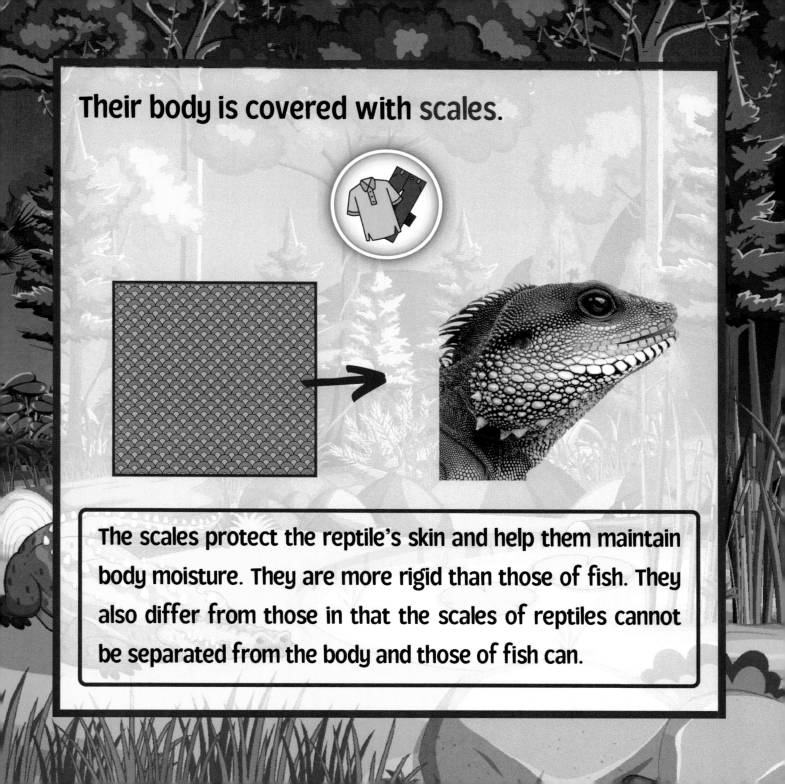

The scales protect the reptile's skin and help them maintain body moisture. They are more rigid than those of fish. They also differ from those in that the scales of reptiles cannot be separated from the body and those of fish can.

SUMMARY

- They are oviparous.

- They breathe through their lungs.

- They are cold-blooded.

- They have their body covered with scales.

- They are terrestrial animals.

DID YOU KNOW...?

- Despite their bad reputation, most snakes are not poisonous. But beware of the ones that are!

- Reptiles tend to live for many years. Jonathan the tortoise, from the Seychelles islands, reached the age of 190 in 2022.

- The saltwater crocodile can measure more than 20 ft (6 m) and weigh more than a ton.

- The longest snake in the world is the reticulated python. It measures about 20 ft (6 m) in length, although specimens of almost 31 ft (10 m) have been found.

- The largest lizard is the Komodo dragon. It measures 10 ft (3 m) on average and weighs about 154 lb (70 kg).

We have now reached the end

Without a doubt, the world of vertebrate animals is full of amazing things.

Every year new things are learned about them also even new species are discovered. It will be interesting to know what new data we will collect, from now on, from this great family of which we are a small part.

I want to ask you a favor so that this book reaches more people, and that is that you rate it with a sincere opinion on the platform where you purchased it.

With that small gesture, you will be helping me to carry on with new projects.

I can't wait to start creating my next book for you!

You can leave your review directly here. It will only take you a few seconds.

www.amzn.to/3uuM4pA

SCAN ME

Thank you in advance for taking time to share your experience. I appreciate your support!

See you soon!

KEEP LEARNING WITH OUR EDUCATIONAL CHILDREN'S BOOKS

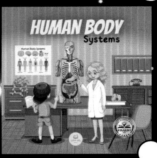

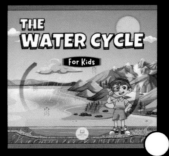

SCAN ME

https://www.pge.me/childrensbooks

Subscribe to my newsletter, receive 4 FREE BONUS, and stay informed of new publications, offers, and promotions of free books.

www.subscribepage.io/ebookfree

Bonus #1 - Free ebook "The The Steadfast Tin Soldier"
Bonus #2 - 19 Printable Halloween Coloring Pages
Bonus #3 - 50 Printable Mazes With Solutions
Bonus #4 - Free ebook With Sample Pages

Samuel John

BOOKS

🛒 https://www.pge.me/childrensbooks

✉️ contacto@samueljohnbooks.com

f www.facebook.com/bookssamueljohn/

FOLLOW ME

www.amazon.com/author/samueljohnbooks

Made in United States
Orlando, FL
02 April 2024